JENNIFER

Shown on Front Cover.

◼◻◻ **EASY**

FINISHED SIZE: Adult [22" (56 cm) circumference]

MATERIALS
Medium/Worsted Weight Yarn: 🔵**4** MEDIUM
3 ounces, 140 yards
(90 grams, 128 meters)
Crochet hook, size H (5 mm) **or** size needed
for gauge

GAUGE SWATCH: 3" (7.5 cm) diameter
Work same as Body through Rnd 2.

STITCH GUIDE

FRONT POST TREBLE CROCHET
(abbreviated FPtr)
YO twice, insert hook from **front** to **back**
around post of st indicated *(Fig. 2, page 15)*,
YO and pull up a loop (4 loops on hook),
YO and draw through 2 loops on hook) 3
times. Skip st behind FPtr.

BODY

Ch 4; join with slip st to form a ring.

Rnd 1 (Right side)**:** Ch 3 **(counts as first dc, now and throughout)**, 11 dc in ring; join with slip st to first dc: 12 dc.

Rnd 2: Ch 9 **(counts as first dc plus ch 6)**, dc in same st, skip next dc, ★ (dc, ch 6, dc) in next dc, skip next dc; repeat from ★ around; join with slip st to first dc: 6 ch-6 sps.

Rnd 3: Turn; slip st in next dc and in next ch-6 sp, ch 1, 6 hdc in same sp, ch 2, (6 hdc in next ch-6 sp, ch 2) around; join with slip st to Front Loop Only of first hdc *(Fig. 1, page 15)*: 36 hdc and 6 ch-2 sps.

Rnd 4: Ch 3, turn; working in Back Loops Only, (dc, ch 1, dc) in next ch-2 sp, ★ dc in next 6 hdc, (dc, ch 1, dc) in next ch-2 sp; repeat from ★ around to last 5 hdc, dc in last 5 hdc; join with slip st to first dc: 48 dc and 6 ch-1 sps.

Rnd 5: Ch 1, turn; working in both loops, hdc in first 7 sts, 3 hdc in next ch-1 sp, (hdc in next 8 dc, 3 hdc in next ch-1 sp) around to last dc, hdc in last dc; join with slip st to Front Loop Only of first hdc: 66 hdc.

Rnd 6: Ch 3, turn; working in Back Loops Only, dc in next hdc, working **around** next 3 hdc *(Fig. A)*, (dc, ch 1, dc) in ch-1 sp one rnd **below**, skip 3 hdc just worked around, ★ dc in next 8 hdc, working **around** next 3 hdc, (dc, ch 1, dc) in ch-1 sp one rnd **below**, skip 3 hdc just worked around; repeat from ★ around to last 6 hdc, dc in last 6 hdc; join with slip st to first dc: 60 dc and 6 ch-1 sps.

Fig. A

1

Instructions continued on page 2.

Rnd 7: Ch 1, turn; working in both loops, hdc in first 7 sts, skip next dc, 3 hdc in next ch-1 sp, ★ skip next dc, hdc in next 8 dc, skip next dc, 3 hdc in next ch-1 sp; repeat from ★ around to last 2 dc, skip next dc, hdc in last dc; join with slip st to Front Loop Only of first hdc: 66 hdc.

Rnd 8: Ch 3, turn; working in Back Loops Only, dc in next hdc, working **around** next 3 hdc, (dc, ch 1, dc) in ch-1 sp one rnd **below**, skip 3 hdc just worked around, ★ dc in next 3 hdc, work FPtr around each of next 2 dc one rnd **below**, dc in next 3 hdc, working **around** next 3 hdc, (dc, ch 1, dc) in ch-1 sp one rnd **below**, skip 3 hdc just worked around; repeat from ★ around to last 6 hdc, dc in next 3 hdc, work FPtr around each of next 2 dc one rnd **below**, dc in last hdc; join with slip st to first dc: 60 sts and 6 ch-1 sps.

Rnd 9: Repeat Rnd 7: 66 hdc.

Rnds 10-13: Repeat Rnds 6-9: 66 hdc.

Rnd 14: Ch 1, turn; sc in Back Loop Only of first hdc and each hdc around; join with slip st both loops of first sc.

Rnds 15-17: Ch 1, do **not** turn; sc in both loops of same st and each sc around; join with slip st to first sc.

Finish off.

ASHLEY CAP

Shown on page 5.

■■□□ EASY

FINISHED SIZE: Adult [22" (56 cm) circumference]

MATERIALS

BULKY 5

Bulky Weight Yarn:
    5 ounces, 165 yards
        (140 grams, 151 meters)
    Crochet hook, size G (4 mm) **or** size needed
        for gauge

GAUGE SWATCH: 3³/₄" (9.5 cm) diameter
Work same as Body through Rnd 3.

STITCH GUIDE

BEGINNING POPCORN
Ch 3, 3 dc in same st or sp, drop loop from hook, insert hook in first dc of 4-dc group, hook dropped loop and draw through st.
POPCORN (uses one st or sp)
4 Dc in st or sp indicated, drop loop from hook, insert hook in first dc of 4-dc group, hook dropped loop and draw through st.
BACK POST DOUBLE CROCHET
    (abbreviated BPdc)
YO, insert hook from **back** to **front** around post of st indicated (*Fig. 2, page 15*), YO and pull up a loop (3 loops on hook), (YO and draw through 2 loops on hook) twice.
FRONT POST DOUBLE CROCHET
    (abbreviated FPdc)
YO, insert hook from **front** to **back** around post of dc indicated (*Fig. 2, page 15*), YO and pull up a loop (3 loops on hook), (YO and draw through 2 loops on hook) twice.

ODY

4; join with slip st to form a ring.

d 1 (Right side)**:** Ch 3 **(counts as first dc,**
w and throughout), 11 dc in ring; join with
 st to first dc: 12 dc.

d 2: Work Beginning Popcorn in same st,
 2, working in Back Loops Only *(Fig. 1,*
ge 15), (work Popcorn in next dc, ch 2)
und; join with slip st to top of Beginning
pcorn: 12 Popcorns and 12 ch-2 sps.

d 3: Slip st in next ch-2 sp, ch 3, (2 dc, ch 1,
c) in same sp, dc in next ch-2 sp, ★ (3 dc,
 1, 3 dc) in next ch-2 sp, dc in next ch-2 sp;
eat from ★ around; join with slip st to first dc:
 dc and 6 ch-1 sps.

d 4: Slip st in next 2 dc and in next ch-1 sp,
rk (Beginning Popcorn, ch 2, Popcorn) in
ne sp, skip next 3 dc, work 6 FPdc around next
 ★ work (Popcorn, ch 2, Popcorn) in next
-1 sp, skip next 3 dc, work 6 FPdc around next
 repeat from ★ around; join with slip st to top
Beginning Popcorn: 36 FPdc, 12 Popcorns, and
h-2 sps.

Rnd 5: Slip st in next ch-2 sp, ch 3, (2 dc, ch 1,
3 dc) in same sp, work BPdc around each of next
6 FPdc, ★ (3 dc, ch 1, 3 dc) in next ch-2 sp, work
BPdc around each of next 6 FPdc; repeat from ★
around; join with slip st to first dc: 36 dc,
36 BPdc, and 6 ch-1 sps.

Rnd 6: Slip st in next 2 dc and in next ch-1 sp,
work (Beginning Popcorn, ch 2, Popcorn) in
same sp, skip next 3 dc, work BPdc around each
of next 3 BPdc, ch 2, work BPdc around each of
next 3 BPdc, ★ work (Popcorn, ch 2, Popcorn) in
next ch-1 sp, skip next 3 dc, work BPdc around
each of next 3 BPdc, ch 2, work BPdc around
each of next 3 BPdc; repeat from ★ around; join
with slip st to top of Beginning Popcorn:
36 BPdc, 12 Popcorns, and 12 ch-2 sps.

Rnd 7: Slip st in next ch-2 sp, ch 3, (2 dc, ch 1,
3 dc) in same sp, work BPdc around each of next
3 BPdc, ch 2, work BPdc around each of next
3 BPdc, ★ (3 dc, ch 1, 3 dc) in next ch-2 sp,
work BPdc around each of next 3 BPdc, ch 2,
work BPdc around each of next 3 BPdc; repeat
from ★ around; join with slip st to first dc: 36 dc,
36 BPdc, and 12 sps.

Rnds 8-15: Repeat Rnds 6 and 7, 4 times:
36 dc, 36 BPdc, and 12 sps.

Rnd 16: Ch 1, sc in same st, working in Back
Loops Only, sc in next 2 dc, skip next ch-1 sp, sc
in next 6 sts, skip next ch-2 sp, (sc in next 6 sts,
skip next sp) around to last 3 BPdc, sc in last
3 BPdc; join with slip st to first sc: 72 sc.

Rnd 17: Ch 1, sc in Back Loop Only of same st
and each sc around; join with slip st to first sc.

Rnd 18: Ch 1, sc in Back Loop Only of same st
and each sc around; join with slip st to **both**
loops of first sc, finish off.

ETHAN CAP

Shown on page 7.

◧◧◻◻ **EASY**

FINISHED SIZE: Adult [22" (56 cm) circumference]

MATERIALS
Medium/Worsted Weight Yarn: 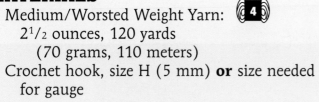 **MEDIUM 4**
   2¹/₂ ounces, 120 yards
      (70 grams, 110 meters)
Crochet hook, size H (5 mm) **or** size needed
   for gauge

GAUGE SWATCH: 2¹/₂" (6.25 cm) diameter
Work same as Body through Rnd 2.

STITCH GUIDE

FRONT POST DOUBLE CROCHET
   (abbreviated FPdc)
YO, insert hook from **front** to **back** around
post of st indicated *(Fig. 2, page 15)*, YO and
pull up a loop (3 loops on hook), (YO and
draw through 2 loops on hook) twice.

BACK POST DOUBLE CROCHET
   (abbreviated BPdc)
YO, insert hook from **back** to **front** around
post of st indicated *(Fig. 2, page 15)*, YO and
pull up a loop (3 loops on hook), (YO and
draw through 2 loops on hook) twice.

BODY

Ch 4; join with slip st to form a ring.

Rnd 1 (Right side)**:** Ch 3 **(counts as first dc,
now and throughout)**, 11 dc in ring; join with
slip st to first dc: 12 dc.

Rnd 2: Ch 3, working in Back Loops Only
(Fig. 1, page 15), dc in same st, 2 dc in next dc
and in each dc around; join with slip st to first
dc: 24 dc.

Rnd 3: Slip st from **front** to **back** around post
of same st *(Fig. 2, page 15)*, ch 3, dc in next dc,
work BPdc around **same** dc, ★ work FPdc around
next dc, dc in next dc, work BPdc around **same**
dc; repeat from ★ around; join with slip st to first
st: 36 sts.

Rnd 4: Ch 1, turn; hdc in first 2 sts, 2 hdc in
next st, (hdc in next 2 sts, 2 hdc in next st)
around; join with slip st to Front Loop Only of
first hdc: 48 hdc.

Rnd 5: Ch 3, turn; working in Back Loops Only
dc in same st and in next 2 hdc, (2 dc in next
hdc, dc in next 2 hdc) around; join with slip st
first dc: 64 dc.

Rnd 6: Do **not** turn; slip st from **front** to **back**
around post of same st, ch 3, work BPdc around
next dc, (work FPdc around next dc, work BPdc
around next dc) around; join with slip st to first
st.

Rnd 7: Ch 1, turn; hdc in first st and in each
around; join with slip st to Front Loop Only of
first hdc.

Rnd 8: Ch 3, turn; dc in Back Loop Only of
next hdc and each hdc around; join with slip st
to first dc.

Rnds 9-16: Repeat Rnds 6-8 twice, then repeat
Rnds 6 and 7 once **more**.

Rnd 17: Ch 1, turn; sc in Back Loop Only of
first hdc and each hdc around; join with slip st
both loops of first sc.

Rnds 18-20: Ch 1, do **not** turn; sc in both
loops of same st and each sc around; join with
slip st to first sc.

Finish off.

JESSICA CAP

Shown on page 10.

◼◼◻◻ **EASY**

FINISHED SIZE: Adult [22" (56 cm) circumference]

MATERIALS
Bulky Weight Yarn: **BULKY 5**
5 ounces, 170 yards
(140 grams, 155 meters)
Crochet hook, size G (4 mm) **or** size needed for gauge

GAUGE SWATCH: 3" (7.5 cm) diameter
Work same as Body through Rnd 2.

STITCH GUIDE

BEGINNING POPCORN
Ch 3, 3 dc in same st, drop loop from hook, insert hook in first dc of 4-dc group, hook dropped loop and draw through st.
POPCORN (uses one st or sp)
4 Dc in st or sp indicated, drop loop from hook, insert hook in first dc of 4-dc group, hook dropped loop and draw through st.

BODY

Ch 4; join with slip st to form a ring

Rnd 1 (Right side)**:** Ch 3 **(counts as first dc, now and throughout)**, 11 dc in ring; join with slip st to first dc: 12 dc.

Rnd 2: Work Beginning Popcorn, ch 2, (work Popcorn in next dc, ch 2) around; join with slip st to top of Beginning Popcorn: 12 ch-2 sps.

Rnd 3: Slip st in first ch-2 sp, ch 3, (dc, ch 1, 2 dc) in same sp, (2 dc, ch 1, 2 dc) in next ch-2 sp and in each ch-2 sp around; join with slip st to first dc: 48 dc and 12 ch-1 sps.

Rnd 4: Slip st in next dc and in next ch-1 sp, ch 1, 3 sc in same sp, ch 1, (5 sc in next ch-1 sp, ch 1) around, 2 sc in same sp as first sc; join with slip st to first sc: 60 sc and 12 ch-1 sps.

Rnd 5: Ch 3, (dc, ch 1, 2 dc) in same st, work Popcorn in next ch-1 sp, skip next 2 sc, ★ (2 dc, ch 1, 2 dc) in next sc, work Popcorn in next ch-1 sp, skip next 2 sc; repeat ★ from around; join with slip st to first dc: 48 dc, 12 Popcorns, and 12 ch-1 sps.

Rnds 6-12: Slip st in next dc and in next ch-1 sp, ch 3, (dc, ch 1, 2 dc) in same sp, work Popcorn in next Popcorn, ★ (2 dc, ch 1, 2 dc) next ch-1 sp, work Popcorn in next Popcorn; repeat from ★ around; join with slip st to first

Rnd 13: Ch 1, sc in same st and in each st an each ch-1 sp around; join with slip st to first sc 72 sc.

Rnds 14-16: Ch 1, sc in same st and in each around; join with slip st to first sc.

Finish off.

8

DAKOTA CAP

...own on page 11.

■■□□ EASY

FINISHED SIZE: Adult [22" (56 cm) circumference]

MATERIALS

Bulky Weight Yarn:
  2¹/₂ ounces, 90 yards
    (70 grams, 82.5 meters)
Crochet hook, size G (4 mm) **or** size needed
  for gauge

GAUGE SWATCH: 3¹/₄" (8.25 cm) diameter
Work same as Body through Rnd 3.

BODY

Ch 4; join with slip st to form a ring.

Rnd 1 (Right side): Ch 3 **(counts as first dc)**,
... dc in ring; join with slip st to first dc: 12 dc.

Rnd 2: Ch 4 **(counts as first dc plus ch 1,
now and throughout)**, (dc in next dc, ch 1)
around; join with slip st to first dc: 12 ch-1 sps.

Rnd 3: Ch 1, turn; slip st in first ch-1 sp, ch 1,
hdc in same sp and in each ch-1 sp around;
join with slip st to Front Loop Only of first hdc
(Fig. 1, page 15): 36 hdc.

Rnd 4: Ch 4, turn; working in Back Loops Only,
skip next hdc, 2 dc in next hdc, ★ dc in next hdc,
ch 1, skip next hdc, 2 dc in next hdc; repeat from
★ around; join with slip st to first dc:
... ch-1 sps.

Rnd 5: Ch 1, turn; working in both loops, (hdc
in next 3 dc, 3 hdc in next ch-1 sp) around; join
with slip st to Front Loop Only of first hdc:
... hdc.

Rnd 6: Ch 4, turn; working in Back Loops Only,
skip next hdc, ★ dc in next hdc, ch 1, skip next
hdc; repeat from ★ around; join with slip st to
first dc: 36 dc and 36 ch-1 sps.

Rnd 7: Ch 1, turn; 2 hdc in first ch-1 sp and in
each ch-1 sp around; join with slip st to Front
Loop Only of first hdc: 72 hdc.

Rnds 8-13: Repeat Rnds 6 and 7, 3 times:
72 hdc.

Rnd 14: Ch 1, turn; sc in Back Loop Only of
first hdc and each hdc around; join with slip st to
both loops of first sc.

Rnds 15-17: Ch 1, do **not** turn; sc in both
loops of same st and each sc around; join with
slip st to first sc.

Finish off.